"She just wants the hot wax!"

Other Herman Books

The 1st Treasury of Herman

The Second Herman Treasury

Herman, The Third Treasury

Herman: The Fourth Treasury

Herman Treasury 5

Herman, The Sixth Treasury

Herman Over the Wall: The Seventh Treasury

"Herman, Dinner's Served. . .
as Soon as the Smoke Clears!"

Herman, You Were a Much Stronger
Man on Our First Honeymoon

The Latest Herman

"Herman, You Can Get in the Bathroom Now"

"They're Gonna Settle Out of Court, Herman"

"She just wants the hot wax!"

by Jim Unger

Andrews and McMeel
A Universal Press Syndicate Company
Kansas City

"I'll be wearing a pink carnation."

"That's a photograph of my wife's mother with the lens cap on."

"I can't be any fairer than that—
$1.5 million reduced to $25."

"Don't keep complaining about my mother."

"Smoking or non-smoking?"

"The doctor says your cast can come off as soon as you've paid."

"'Catch of the day' is off till the fog clears."

8

"Someone spilled a bottle this morning."

"Look at that rustproofing."

"They knew how to build skeletons in those days."

"You're exactly the same size as me."

10

"First, a light dusting of defoliant."

"They know it's feeding time in 10 minutes."

11

"This hammer keeps hitting two inches to the left."

"He's so lazy. He bought himself an exercise car."

12

"Settle an argument. How do you pronounce his name?"

"We can't stand the sight of each other."

"You wouldn't last five minutes where I come from."

"Table for two. Food for five."

14

"He's not very sociable."

"Shall I do one for my wife while I'm here?"

"Well, at least the trip's over."

"I can't move my head."

"Imagine you've got 12 of these babies
and a burglar breaks in."

"Modern technology . . . 47 floors in six seconds."

"How do you expect me to average 55 miles an hour if I don't speed?"

"I don't need to learn reading. It's all on TV."

18

"Whatever that was. I'll have another one."

"That's more like it — 127 pounds."

19

"I lost the five grand. What's our next step?"

"I thought it was you."

"He's a long-haired terrier."

"If your name's on this list, they're out."

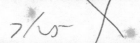

"I'm not late. I was giving you a little 'wait training.'"

"He had an emergency operation."

"It's just till I fix the hole in our fence."

"I'll give you directions. Just don't drive above jogging speed."

"Your baggage arrived, but your wife
went to Tokyo."

"If I was a tipper, you'd definitely get one."

24

"Looks all right to me."

"I asked my new secretary to get me a sheet of graph paper."

25

"I think you've had enough. Why don't I call you a cab?"

"He doesn't need pockets."

26

"I just wanted to tell you I'm gonna be late."

"I missed my dentist's appointment."

27

"Can I borrow your ashtray?"

"I could have left you a tip if you hadn't talked me into that cheesecake."

28

"Everyone at work drew straws and we lost."

"I don't want a son-in-law who's stupid enough to marry my daughter."

29

"Give the ticket to my husband.
He taught me to drive."

"What have you got within walking distance?"

"Makes you wonder how we ever managed without it."

31

"I wanna be able to breathe if I sink."

"That sign wasn't there when you went in."

"We bought you two toasters in case things don't work out."

"Is this kid yours?"

33

"I want to make sure nobody steps on him."

"I can get to the supermarket in under six minutes."

"Can you tell me how to get to Wimpole Lane, Berry Street, Tunney Crescent and Orchard Park Avenue?"

"I'll hand you over to our washroom specialist."

35

"This must be the middle of nowhere."

"What did I tell you, the guy in the bow tie won."

36

"If you hadn't been hiding in the bushes,
I wouldn't have been speeding."

"They just seized a truckload of government toilet
seats. The estimated street value is $2 billion."

"I'm leaving this for income tax just in case I get caught."

"Can I help it if your birthday coincides with the electricity bill?"

"I knew my little girl would leave one day.
That's how I've kept my sanity."

"I wrote you love letters before we were married
because I could afford stamps."

"I've decided to give you another chance.
Next time case the joint first."

"He loves Chinese food."

40

"When I shout 'Gun,' duck."

"I only just made it out of the last place."

"Where does he take the driving test?"

"That suit was made for you. It's the cheapest one we've got."

42

"One of these is a prescription and one a receipt from a Chinese restaurant."

"I've started my own space program. I've already thrown out her mother."

43

"You're going to have to stop eating on the run."

"Keep whistling. I forgot my glasses."

"She wants something that you don't use."

"Root canal? You've charged me for the Suez Canal."

45

"We've agreed on an out-of-court settlement until
we can each afford a lawyer."

"Do you want an appointment for tomorrow?"

"Do you seriously expect me to hurtle through the air at 30,000 feet and not smoke?"

"My money's on him."

"What's 13 hours off 65 years?"

"Your grandfather . . . has left you . . . his bicycle."

"D'you mind if I sit on that side?
I'm deaf in my right ear."

"Pass the ketchup and one of your sausages."

"It works better than 'Stop.'"

"Fifty-four cents in change, a book of matches
and a bottle opener."

"I don't want to learn to drive — I want to learn to better criticize my husband."

"If you want me to take them after meals, you'd better give me some of my $40 back."

"It's a par-12 til the groundskeeper
gets his back pay."

"Do you sell those invisible hearing aids?"

"We'll have to do another one when the fog clears."

"I don't know how long I've been waiting.
He's got my watch."

"Put 62 cents' worth in there."

"I just asked you how the meat loaf was."

"The population of the Earth grew by 14,000 while you were searching for that nickel."

BAKERY

"That's 'ozone layer cake.'"

"People couldn't spell very good in those days."

"Leave your fax number and we'll let you know."

"Have you got anything for indigestion?"

"My wife needs plenty of warning with the lemonade."

"Any escapes today?"

"Not quite everything."

"Are there any side effects to these pills apart from bankruptcy?"

"Your flight left two hours early owing to a malfunction in the captain's watch."

"George is a big game hunter."

"Can't you remember your number?"

Erthu w/10 or W

"Alex . . . come up this end."

Eith W/W or W/13

"Why don't you try it out before you buy it?"

"It's from the landlord."

"Two rolls of anything. It's for our bedroom."

"You the guy with the fly in his soup?"

"That's in case you run a red light."

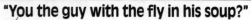

64

"Can you manage that lot in one night?"

"I'm sorry, we do not lend Miss Perkins."

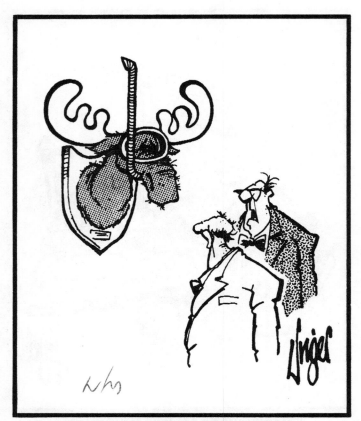

"He almost made it across the river."

"I can't hear any problems, but that's not surprising."

"Anyone else for the airport?"

"You are two completely different personalities.
That'll be 75 bucks each."

"Dad, can I borrow the car payment?"

"It always speeds up when I take my clothes off."

"That's your organic shampoo."

"These should make you relax. You won't have any money to do anything else."

"We'll take the one on the left."

"Taxi!"

"I see the police got your car back."

"Just imagine I'm a pizza and deliver me to my sister's."

Eh 1/w 1/03

"It draws attention away from your face."

"Got any roller skates with airbags?"

"I decided to save you the trouble of visiting me."

"I'm looking for a card that reflects me . . . cheap."

"I hear you're not completely satisfied with your semi-private accommodation."

"I think our popularity is slipping."

74

"It's happy hour. You get two mushroom soups."

"She got a black belt after her first lesson."

"The nurse says you're having trouble
getting out of bed."

"I'm a singing birthday card. Got a piano and
a couple of beers?"

"She's gonna spend my $18 tax refund
on a $400 coat."

"The big ones are 15 years."

77

"That picture was taken when I was on the ground."

"That's 25 cents for the price list and a dollar for the coffee."

"He's probably held up in traffic."

"I opened 13 dummy corporations —
now I can't find my money."

"Sitting Bull's taken the saloon."

"Tachometer for an '89 Ferrari."

"Catch of the day from the wine cellar, Francine."

"I *told* you what 'park' meant."

"I made it out of soap."

"I can't keep anything down."

"There's an escargot in my lettuce."

"Hand over your pacemaker."

"The honeymoon suite just became available."

"One owner."

"I suppose you know you've been standing there for over an hour and the toaster's not plugged in."

"You'll have power steering if your wife drives."

"Tell 'im."

"Just keep going left. If I'm [...] get back, ask so[...]"

"It s[...]"

3/7 3/8

ates quite clearly ... 'evening dress.'"

"With this $365 ring, plus sales tax, I thee wed."

"One cola, no ice."

"Table for one near someone ha

"Would I have worn this hat if I was gonna smuggle?"

"Just how fast were you driving?"

"My candidate is determined to slash spending."

"I've decided to move you up the ladder. Get a bucket."

"If this is 2 percent milk, how much am I paying for the other 98 percent?"

"It's not my fault you're stupid."

"Are these cornflakes biodegradable?"

"Oh yeah? Well, I just may not be there when you get home!"

"And, of course, this model does have the folding bicycle."

4/10

"Pin these up in the kitchen and we won't have any mistakes."

4/11 nr 13

"Next time we'll get a taller plumber."

"Bend your knees."

"I don't care if it does work! Put it back the way it was."

"We're waiting for a probation report, Your Honor."

"Let me write you a check for the other 40 cents."

"Don't get too close. Remember what happened at the zoo."

"Did you have to hang the food right above the tent?"

"Take the next left . . . and what's
the capital of Yugoslavia?"

"You're eating too much sugar."

"Is there any truth to the rumor that you're thinking of retiring from the ring?"

"A picture's supposed to speak a thousand words. I can think of only one."

"That's just in case you drop him."

"I've decided to try shock treatment."

"Get going. I want a dollar's worth around the neighborhood."

"The body fits him, but the neck's too tight."

"Maybe it was ivory poachers."

2/3/80

"Herman, don't go out during thunderstorms."

7/4/90

"I think I'll wear it like this. Then you won't have to keep reminding me how much it cost."